USING YOUR SKILLS

Maths

illustrated by Graham Round

CONTENTS

Ladybird

SIMPLE ADDITION

Jamie and May are going to visit Jamie's uncle, Count Backula, at his haunted house. Here is the map he has given them.

GHOSTLY GUIDANCE

Here is a number line showing all the numbers from 0 to 25. Use it to help you work out the answers by counting on, for example:

Add the number of houses on Back Street to the number of red doors on Side Street.

There are 15 houses on Back Street, so go to 15 on the number line. There are 3 red doors on Side Street, so starting from 15, count on 3 to give you the answer. 15 + 3 = 18.

0 1 2 3 4 5 6 7 8 9 10 11 12 13 14 15 16 17 18 19 20 21 22 23 24 25

Add together the number of:

1 green doors on Hammer Square ______ +
shops on High Street ______ = ______

2 green doors on Side Street ______ +
shops on High Street ______ = ______

3 houses on Hammer Square ______ +
blue doors on Side Street ______ = ______

4 pink houses on Back Street ______ +
red doors on Side Street ______ = ______

5 blue doors on Back Street ______ +
blue doors on Hammer Square ______ +
blue doors on Side Street ______ = ______

ADDITION WITH MONEY

On their way to the house, Jamie and May stop at the ghost-busting shop to buy a spook-zapper – these are the only way to deal with midnight menaces!

Help Jamie and May to work out which coins they need to buy all the parts that make a zapper.

1. 10p + 10p + 10p + ____ p = 32p
2. 2p + 50p + ____ p + 10p = 67p
3. 20p + ____ p + 1p + 20p = 42p
4. 50p + 20p + 10p + ____ p = 81p
5. ____ p + 20p + 5p + 1p = 76p

How much does a spook-zapper cost all together?

£__.____

6 The shop has some pretend spooks so that Jamie and May can test their spook-zapper.

When the spook-clouds are zapped, the numbers fall apart. Rearrange each number to make the biggest number possible. Write the number in the puddle below the correct cloud.

7 Now arrange the numbers in order, starting with the smallest.

8 Which was the biggest number that you made?

GHOSTLY GUIDANCE

Look at the number 832:

8	3	2
The 8 tells you how many HUNDREDS	The 3 tells you how many TENS	The 2 tells you how many UNITS

So, 832 is made up of
8 hundreds and 3 tens and 2 units

$800 + 30 + 2 = 832$

PLACE VALUE

1 Count Backula is tidying up his collections, ready for when Jamie and May arrive. His mummies are hundreds of years old.
How many hundreds are there in each of these numbers?

376 ☐ hundreds **750** ☐ hundreds **912** ☐ hundreds

495 ☐ hundreds **824** ☐ hundreds **124** ☐ hundreds

Put the mummies in order, starting with the oldest.

☐ ☐ ☐ ☐ ☐ ☐

2 Count Backula collects strange boxes. He keeps a record of how old each one is. The tens column will tell you which is the oldest.

Put the boxes in order, starting with the oldest.

☐ ☐ ☐

☐ ☐ ☐

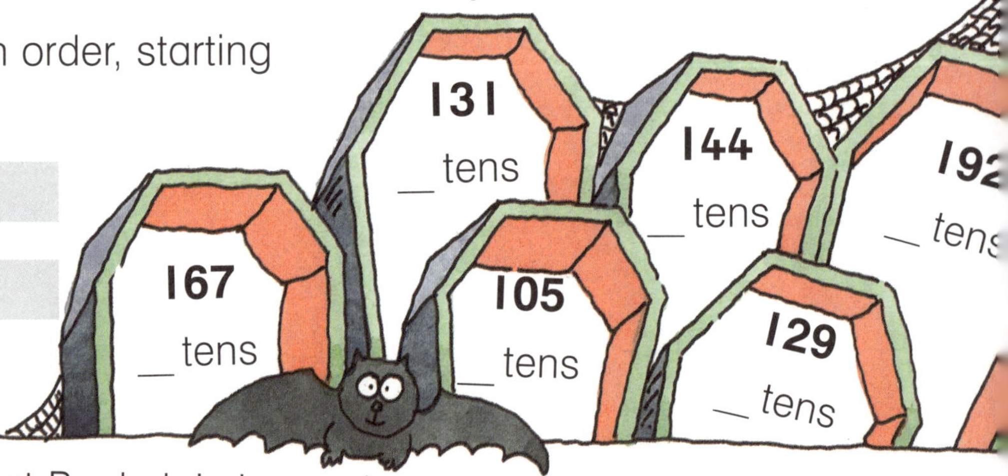

3 Each room in Count Backula's house has about the same number of bats. Write down how many units there are in each of these numbers.

The living room has **65** bats ☐ units The kitchen has **69** bats ☐ uni

The bedroom has **63** bats ☐ units The hall has **61** bats ☐ units

Put the units in order, starting with the smallest. ☐ ☐ ☐ ☐

Which room has most bats? ____________

Now Count Backula is looking out into his garden. He wants to add up all the snakes, rats and worms that live there.

4
$$\begin{array}{r} 23 \\ 23+ \\ \hline \\ \hline \end{array}$$

5
$$\begin{array}{r} 41 \\ 15+ \\ \hline \\ \hline \end{array}$$

6
$$\begin{array}{r} 52 \\ 17+ \\ \hline \\ \hline \end{array}$$

7
$$\begin{array}{r} 45 \\ 32+ \\ \hline \\ \hline \end{array}$$

8
$$\begin{array}{r} 61 \\ 27+ \\ \hline \\ \hline \end{array}$$

9
$$\begin{array}{r} 25 \\ 34+ \\ \hline \\ \hline \end{array}$$

10
$$\begin{array}{r} 123 \\ 432+ \\ \hline \\ \hline \end{array}$$

11
$$\begin{array}{r} 236 \\ 152+ \\ \hline \\ \hline \end{array}$$

SIMPLE SUBTRACTION

Count Backula loves subtractions. He likes to try to catch people out by using different words such as:

TAKE AWAY SUBTRACT MINUS DIFFERENCE

But they all mean that he is taking one number away from another.

$$\begin{array}{r} 15 \\ 3- \\ \hline 12 \end{array}$$

15 take away 3 equals 12
subtract 3 from 15 to leave 12
15 minus 3 equals 12
(15,3) → 12: the difference between 15 and 3 equals 12

Say these subtractions aloud and work out the answers. Then write the whole subtraction using words and numbers in the four different ways that Count Backula uses.

1 $\begin{array}{r} 43 \\ 12- \\ \hline \_\_ \end{array}$

2 $\begin{array}{r} 45 \\ 34- \\ \hline \_\_ \end{array}$

3 $\begin{array}{r} 27 \\ 27- \\ \hline \_\_ \end{array}$

Now Count Backula wants to clear some of the moths, spiders and mice from his workshop.
How many of them has he left behind?

4 $10-3=$ ___
$(7,4) \rightarrow$ ___
11 minus 6 = ___

5 $7-3=$ ___
$(17,3) \rightarrow$ ___
15 minus 8 = ___

6 $8-3=$ ___
$(12,7) \rightarrow$ ___
17 minus 9 = ___

7 $9-3=$ ___
$(8,6) \rightarrow$ ___
13 minus 7 = ___

8 $5-3=$ ___
$(20,4) \rightarrow$ ___
9 minus 3 = ___

9 $6-3=$ ___
$(19,12) \rightarrow$ ___
19 minus 11 = ___

10 T U
32
20-
___
___

11 T U
20
10-
___
___

12 T U
15
5-
___
___

13 T U
97
45-
___
___

GHOSTLY GUIDANCE

Look at the number line showing all the numbers from 0 to 40.

Use it to help you work out the answers by counting back.

For example, to find 37 − 5, start at 37 on the number line and count back 5. This brings you to 32, so 37 − 5 = 32.

14 T U
63
12-
___
___

15 T U
59
37-
___
___

16 T U
57
31-
___
___

17 T U
84
14-
___
___

1 2 3 4 5 6 7 8 9 10 11 12 13 14 15 16 17 18 19 20 21 22 23 24 25 26 27 28 29 30 31 32 33 34 35 36 37 38 39 40

COUNTING ON AND COUNTING BACK GAME

Jamie and May have reached the 39 steps that lead to Count Backula's house. Using a dice and a counter, help them climb the steps to reach the front door. Follow the instructions on each square. Watch out for step 13 – it's the trap door to Count Backula's dungeon! If you fall through it then you have to go back to the start.

19
20 Go back one
21
22
23 Add on ten
24 Go back two then add on eleven
25
26
27
28 Add on eleven
29 Go back Seven
30
31
32
33 Add one
34
35
36 Go back three
37
38
39 Go back twenty-six

REPEATED ADDITION AND MULTIPLICATION

Jamie and May find Count Backula in the hall with his three pet bats. Each bat has two wings. How many wings do they have altogether?

You could write this as a long sum: $2 + 2 + 2 = 6$

or you could write it like this: 3 lots of $2 = 6$

or, even quicker: $3 \times 2 = 6$

Count Backula's rats each have four legs. If there are five rats, how many legs are there altogether? $5 \times 4 = 20$

GHOSTLY GUIDANCE

So that tables don't drive you batty, use this multiplication square to help you find the answers.

X	1	2	3	4	5	6	7	8	9	10
1	1	2	3	4	5	6	7	8	9	10
2	2	4	6	8	10	12	14	16	18	20
3	3	6	9	12	15	18	21	24	27	30
4	4	8	12	16	20	24	28	32	36	40
5	5	10	15	20	25	30	35	40	45	50
6	6	12	18	24	30	36	42	48	54	60
7	7	14	21	28	35	42	49	56	63	70
8	8	16	24	32	40	48	56	64	72	80
9	9	18	27	36	45	54	63	72	81	90
10	10	20	30	40	50	60	70	80	90	100

Count Backula is counting how many bats there are in the corners of each room in his house. Can you help him?

1. 4 x 1 =
2. 2 x 3 =
3. 4 x 3 =
4. 6 x 6 =
5. 7 x 4 =
6. 3 x 7 =
7. 6 x 2 =
8. 5 x 3 =
9. 7 x 2 =
10. 4 x 4 =
11. 5 x 5 =
12. 6 x 7 =
13. 6 x 4 =
14. 4 x 5 =
15. 2 x 8 =
16. 5 x 8 =
17. 9 x 3 =
18. 7 x 8 =

MULTIPLICATION TRIANGLES

Count Backula has set Jamie and May some puzzles that they must solve before they can find him.

Here is an example.
Can you see how it works?

The numbers in the circles are multiplied together to give the numbers in the squares.

Practise with these before solving Count Backula's puzzle.

COUNT BACKULA'S PUZZLE

Here is a plan of Count Backula's house. Write the missing numbers in each multiplication triangle, then work out the correct name for each room. The missing numbers are clues to the names of the rooms.

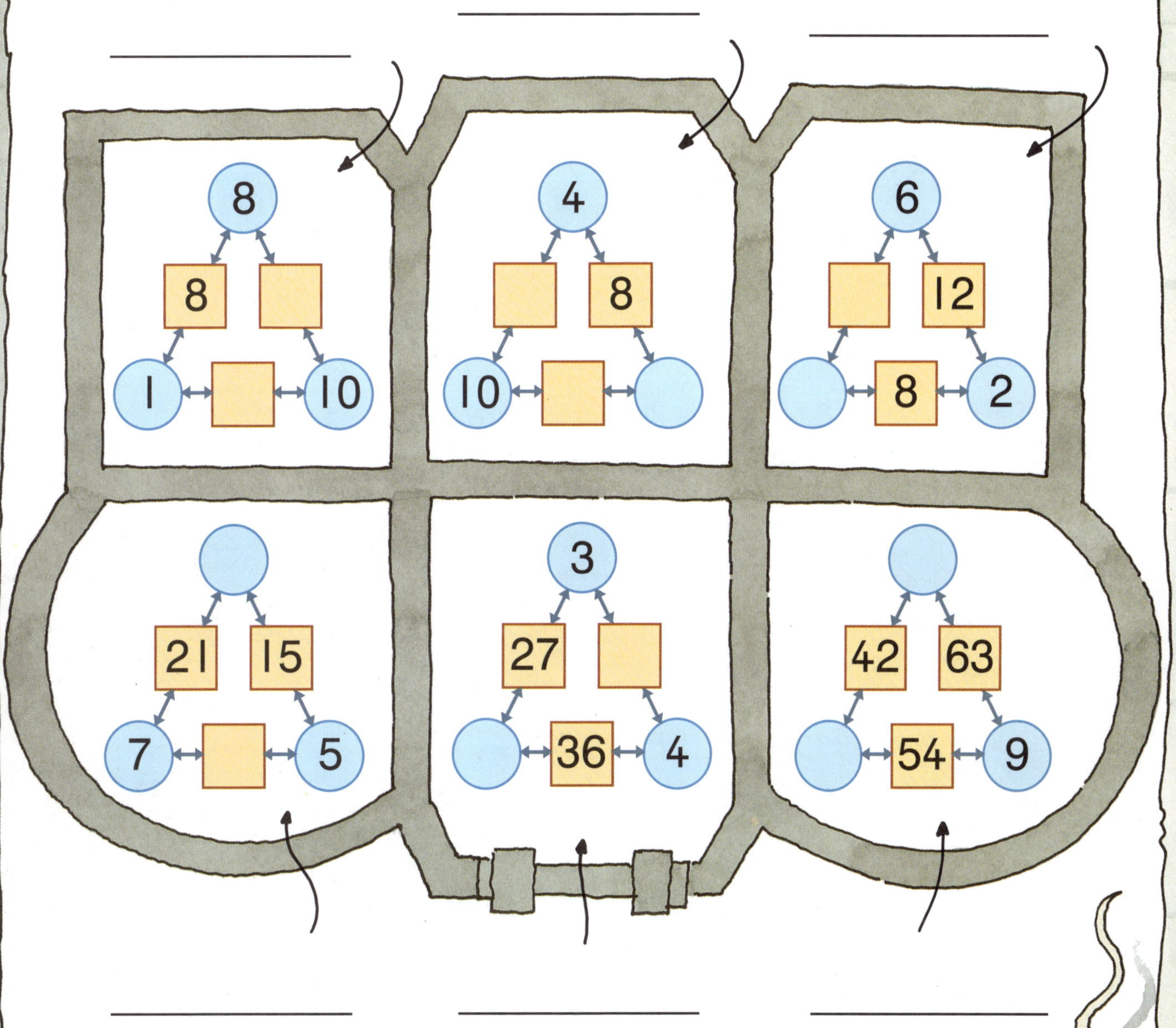

Some of the **missing** numbers are:

Kitchen = 7

Living room = 24

Bedroom = 80

Hall = 9

Dungeon = 3

Attic = 20

SHARING AND DIVISION

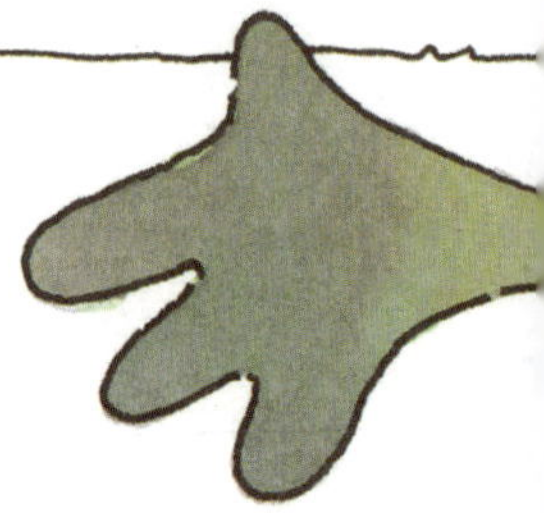

The three ghosts that haunt Count Backula's house don't like to be in the same room as one another. Look at the plan of Count Backula's house to see how the ghosts have shared the house between them.

There are six rooms in total.

Ghoul haunts the bedroom and the attic = 2 rooms

Spook haunts the living room and the kitchen = 2 rooms

Spectre haunts the dungeon and the hall = 2 rooms

So,
6 rooms shared between **3** ghosts means that there are **2** rooms each.

This can be written as a division sum:

$6 \div 3 = 2$

Now try these division sums.

1 $16 \div 4 =$	5 $15 \div 5 =$	9 $14 \div 2 =$
2 $4 \div 2 =$	6 $16 \div 8 =$	10 $12 \div 6 =$
3 $12 \div 3 =$	7 $20 \div 4 =$	11 $6 \div 2 =$
4 $36 \div 6 =$	8 $24 \div 4 =$	12 $30 \div 5 =$

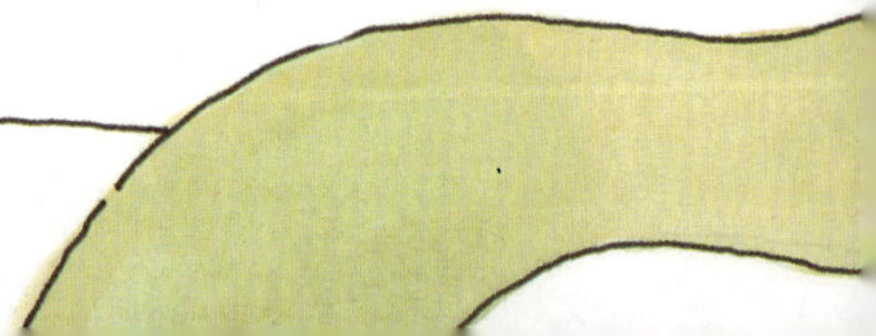

If Count Backula built another room on to his house, the ghosts would not be able to share the whole house equally. There would be one room left over that was not haunted.

So, **7** rooms shared between **3** ghosts would mean that there are **2** rooms each with **1** room left over:

$7 \div 3 = 2$ remainder 1.

Try these division sums, writing in the answer and the remainder for each – **rem** is short for remainder. The first one is done for you.

13 $13 \div 3 = 4$ rem 1

14 $18 \div 7 =$ rem

15 $24 \div 5 =$ rem

16 $9 \div 2 =$ rem

17 $11 \div 2 =$ rem

18 $23 \div 4 =$ rem

19 $15 \div 4 =$ rem

20 $25 \div 6 =$ rem

21 $10 \div 3 =$ rem

22 $17 \div 5 =$ rem

23 $17 \div 8 =$ rem

24 $10 \div 1 =$ rem

25 $16 \div 7 =$ rem

26 $7 \div 3 =$ rem

SHAPES AND SIZES

To help them haunt, Count Backula's ghosts can make themselves into any shape they like.

Ghoul has made himself square-shaped.

He has four sides of equal length.

Measure one side with a ruler.

One side of the square measures   centimetres.

Without measuring the other sides, how far is it to go round all four sides?

4 x ___ = ___ cm

The distance all round the edge of a shape is called the **perimeter**.

Measure the perimeter (to the nearest half centimetre) of all the shapes that Ghoul and the other ghosts have formed.

Write the answers inside each shape.

TIME

Count Backula has to keep a close eye on his clocks. He needs to know exactly when to get up at night and exactly when to go to bed in the mornings. Can you help him to find out what time it is? Draw the hands on these clocks.

GHOSTLY GUIDANCE

Remember, the long hand of a watch is called the minute hand. It takes five minutes to move from one number to the next. Use these clocks to help you.

When the long hand is moving between the 12 and the 6, it is showing how many minutes past the hour.

What time is shown on these clocks?

1 ______________

2 ______________

3 ______________

4 ______________

5 ______________

6 ______________

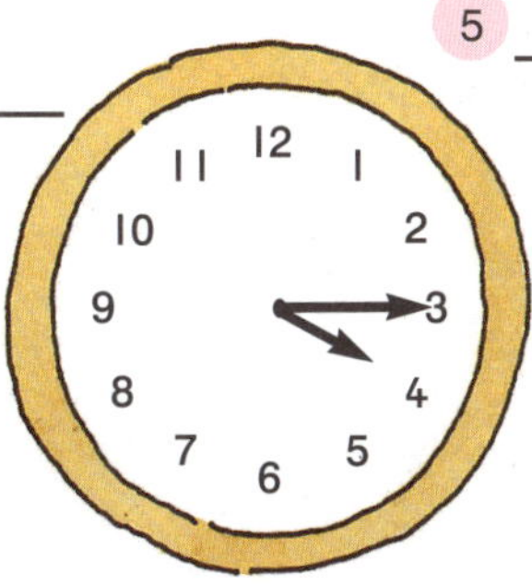

7 ______________

8 ______________

9 ______________

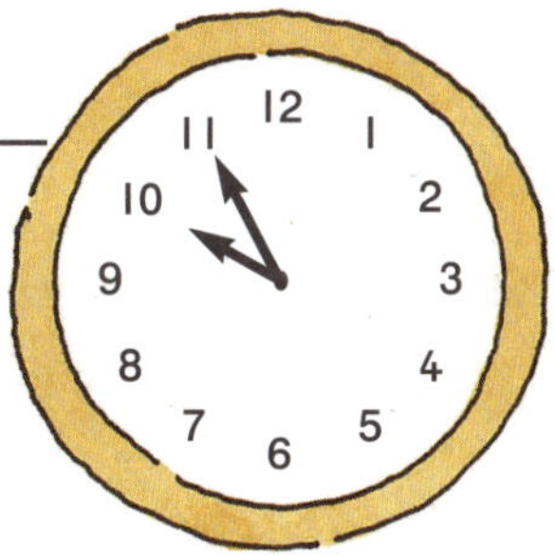

10 ______________

11 ______________

When the long hand is moving between the 6 and the 12, it is showing how many minutes to the next hour.

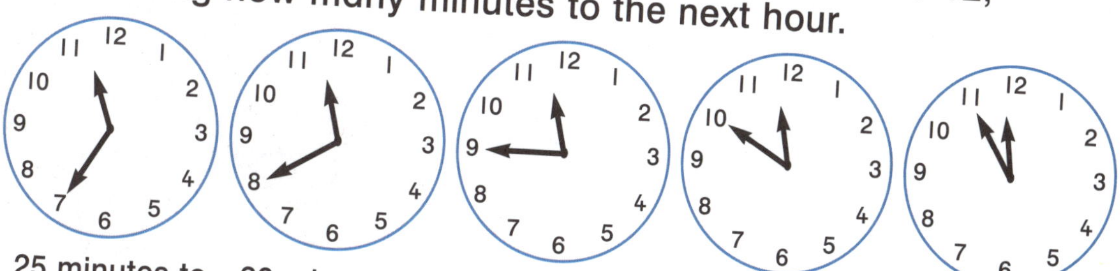

25 minutes to | **20 minutes to** | **15 minutes (quarter) to** | **10 minutes to** | **5 minutes to**

CO-ORDINATES

Here is a map of the Count's garden.

The shaking shed is in square (4,2). This means that it can be found four squares across and two squares up.

The numbers across and up are called **co-ordinates**.

The **across** number is always written **first**.

Help Jamie and May to find all the spooky items in Count Backula's garden.

Shaking shed	(4,2)
Pool of plenty	_____
Trembling tree	_____
Mouldering mound	_____
Magnificent moondial	_____
Whispering grass	_____

Co-ordinates can also be used to write messages in secret code.

5	A	B	C	D	E
4	F	G	H	I	J
3	K	L	M	N	O
2	P	Q Z	R	S	T
1	U	V	W	X	Y
	1	2	3	4	5

Then up ↑

Across first →

B is in square (2,5)

A is in square (1,5)

T is in square (5,2)

So **BAT** written in code is: (2,5) (1,5) (5,2)

Can you work out the message that Count Backula has left for Jamie and May?

(3,4) (1,5) (2,1) (5,5) (5,4) (1,1) (4,2) (5,2)
(1,2) (5,3) (1,2) (1,2) (5,5) (4,5) (5,3) (1,1) (5,2)
(1,4) (5,3) (3,2) (1,5) (2,5) (4,4) (5,2) (5,5)
(2,5) (1,5) (3,5) (1,3) (2,5) (5,5) (1,4) (5,3) (3,2) (5,5)
(4,5) (1,5) (3,1) (4,3)

ANSWERS

PAGE 3

1 7 **2** 13 **3** 21 **4** 5 **5** 23

PAGE 4

1 2p **2** 5p **3** 1p **4** 1p **5** 50p
£2.98

PAGE 5

6 832, 942, 210, 751, 520, 983, 764, 732
7 210, 520, 732, 751, 764, 832, 942, 983 **8** 983

PAGE 6

1 376 = 3 hundreds, 750 = 7 hundreds, 912 = 9 hundreds, 495 = 4 hundreds, 824 = 8 hundreds, 124 = 1 hundred; 912, 824, 750, 495, 376, 124 **2** 131 = 3 tens, 144 = 4 tens, 192 = 9 tens, 167 = 6 tens, 105 = 0 tens, 129 = 2 tens; 192, 167, 144, 131, 129, 105 **3** 65 = 5 units, 69 = 9 units, 63 = 3 units, 61 = 1 unit; 1, 3, 5, 9; in the kitchen

PAGE 7

4 46 **5** 56 **6** 69 **7** 77 **8** 88 **9** 59 **10** 555 **11** 388

PAGE 8

1 43 take away 12 equals 31; subtract 12 from 43 to leave 31; 43 minus 12 equals 31; (43,12) → 31: the difference between 43 and 12 equals 31
2 45 take away 34 equals 11; subtract 34 from 45 to leave 11; 45 minus 34 equals 11; (45,34) → 11: the difference between 45 and 34 equals 11
3 27 take away 27 equals 0; subtract 27 from 27 to leave 0; 27 minus 27 equals 0; (27,27) → 0: the difference between 27 and 27 equals 0

PAGE 9

4 7, 3, 5 **5** 4, 14, 7 **6** 5, 5, 8 **7** 6, 2, 6 **8** 2, 16, 6 **9** 3, 7, 8 **10** 12 **11** 10 **12** 10 **13** 52 **14** 51 **15** 22 **16** 26 **17** 70

PAGE 13

1 4 **2** 6 **3** 12 **4** 36 **5** 28 **6** 21 **7** 12 **8** 15 **9** 14 **10** 16 **11** 25 **12** 42 **13** 24 **14** 20 **15** 16 **16** 40 **17** 27 **18** 56

PAGE 14

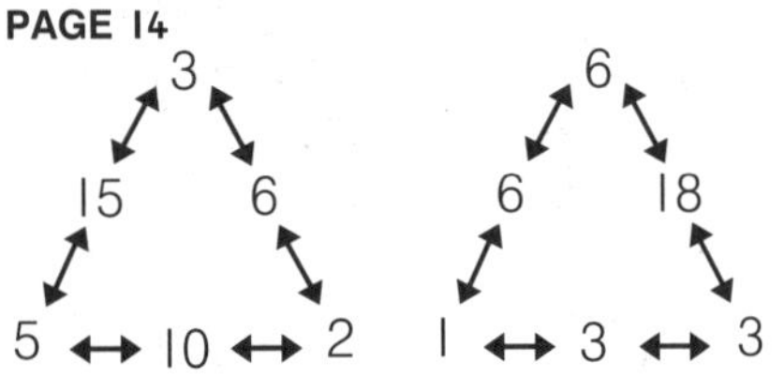

PAGE 15

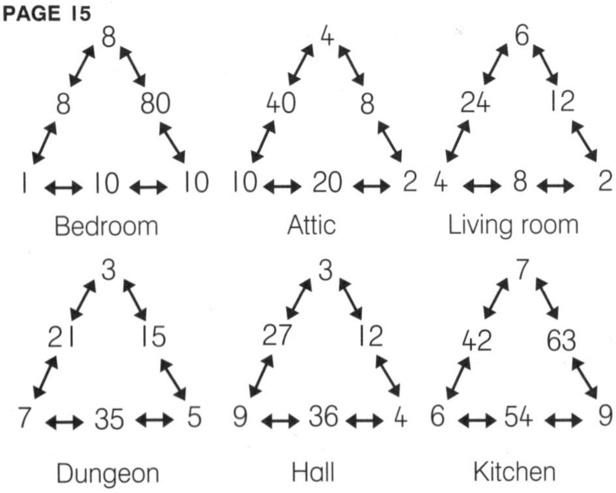

PAGE 16

1 4 **2** 2 **3** 4 **4** 6 **5** 3 **6** 2 **7** 5 **8** 6 **9** 7 **10** 2 **11** 3 **12** 6

PAGE 17

13 4 rem 1 **14** 2 rem 4 **15** 4 rem 4 **16** 4 rem 1
17 5 rem 1 **18** 5 rem 3 **19** 3 rem 3 **20** 4 rem 1
21 3 rem 1 **22** 3 rem 2 **23** 2 rem 1 **24** 10 rem 0
25 2 rem 2 **26** 2 rem 1

PAGE 18

10cm; 4 x 10 = 40 cm

PAGE 19

square 18 cm, *kite* 20 cm, *triangle* 16.5 cm, *octagon* 16 cm, *hexagon* 18 cm, *rectangle* 21 cm, *pentagon* 17.5 cm

PAGE 20

Top row, left to right

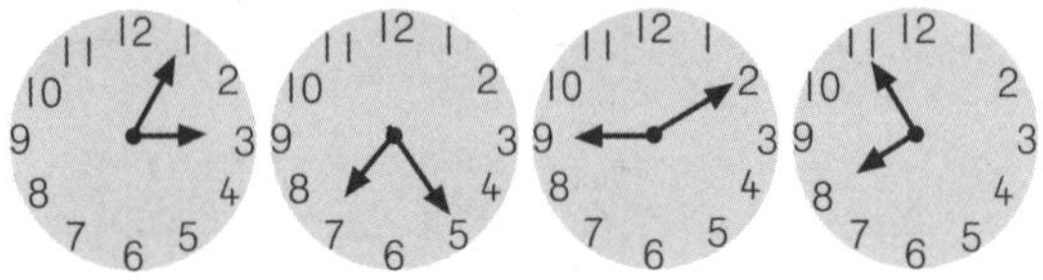

Bottom row, left to right

PAGE 21

1 30 minutes (half) past 6 **2** 25 minutes to 6
3 5 minutes past 2 **4** 20 minutes to 8
5 10 minutes to 8 **6** 20 minutes to 6
7 15 minutes (quarter) past 4 **8** 15 minutes (quarter) to 6 **9** 30 minutes (half) past 10 **10** 5 minutes to 10
11 20 minutes to 11

PAGE 22

Pool of plenty (1,3) *Trembling tree* (2,2)
Mouldering mound (3,1) *Magnificent moondial* (3,4)
Whispering grass (4,4)

PAGE 23

HAVE JUST POPPED OUT FOR A BITE
BACK BEFORE DAWN